The Library of Author Biographies™

Sharon Creech

The Library of Author Biographies™

SHARON CREECH

Alice B. McGinty

The Rosen Publishing Group, Inc., New York

To Sharon

Published in 2006 by The Rosen Publishing Group, Inc.
29 East 21st Street, New York, NY 10010

First Edition

Library of Congress Cataloging-in-Publication Data
McGinty, Alice B., 1963–
Sharon Creech/Alice B. McGinty.—1st ed.
    p. cm.—(The library of author biographies)
Includes bibliographical references and index.
ISBN 1-4042-0468-7 (lib. bdg.)
ISBN 1-4042-0652-3 (pbk. bdg.)
1. Creech, Sharon. 2. Authors, American—20th century—Biography.
3. Children's stories—Authorship. I. Title. II. Series.
PS3553.R3373Z76 2006
813'.54—dc22
                                                    2004030282

Manufactured in the United States of America

Quote from Hendershot, Judith, & Peck, Jacqueline. (1996, February). An interview with Sharon Creech, 1995 Newberry Medal winner. *The Reading Teacher*, 49(5), 380–382. Reprinted with permission of the International Reading Association.
From *St. James Guide to Young Adult Writers*, 2nd Edition, by St. James Press, © 1999, St. James Press. Reprinted by permission of The Gale Group.
From *Beacham's Guide to Literature for Young Adults*, by Beet, Kirk H., and Niemeyer, Suzanne, Gale Group, © 2001, Gale Group. Reprinted by permission of The Gale Group.
From *The Horn Book Magazine*, July/August 1995, and May/June 1997. Reprinted by permission of The Horn Book, Inc., Boston, MA, www.hbook.com.
From *Winning Authors: Profiles of the Newbery Medalists*, Bostrom, Kathleen Long. Copyright © 2003 by Libraries Unlimited. Reproduced with permission of Greenwood Publishing Group, Inc., Westport, CT.
From Lowery-Moore, Hollis. "Creating People Who Are Quirky and Kind: An Interview with Sharon Creech." *Teacher Librarian*, Vol. 28, No. 4 (April 2001), p. 56. Reprinted with permission of Scarecrow Press, Inc.
From *Seventh Book of Junior Authors and Illustrators*, Copyright © 1996, edited by Connie Rockman. Reprinted with permission of The H. W. Wilson Company
From Review of *Bloomability, Booklist* (September 15, 1998), and from Review of *Ruby Holler, Booklist* (April 1, 2002), Copyright © American Library Association. Used with permission.
©1994 VNU Business Media, Inc. Reprinted with permission from Kirkus Reviews.
Excerpt from *Walk Two Moons*. ©1994 by Sharon Creech. Excerpt from *The Wanderer*. ©2000 by Sharon Creech. Used with the permission of HarperCollins Children's Books.

Table of Contents

Introduction: Take a Journey

C ome and take a journey. Sail in a boat across the Atlantic Ocean. Follow a long and winding highway to Lewiston, Idaho. Take in the view from a mountaintop in Switzerland. You don't need to pack a suitcase. No plane fare is required. Just open one of Sharon Creech's books and begin the adventure.

Creech remembers her early journeys—family vacations where she was in awe with the wide world she saw around her. When she was an adult, she wanted to give her children the same opportunity, so she took a job teaching at an American high school in England. Sharon has since moved back to the United States and still enjoys traveling. She loves the excitement of discovering new places, meeting interesting people, and finding out about different ways of life.

Because she was busy teaching, traveling, and raising her children, Sharon Creech did not begin to write books until she was about forty years old. When her young adult novel *Walk Two Moons* was published in 1994, Creech was still teaching high school in England. *Walk Two Moons* was her first book published in the United States. Because of this, the children's literature community did not know who she was. Imagine the surprise that came when *Walk Two Moons* was awarded the 1995 Newbery Medal—the most prestigious award given to a children's book each year in the United States. Librarians, teachers, and readers experienced the joy of new discovery when they read *Walk Two Moons* and knew they'd found a talented new author with a gift for storytelling.

Since her initial breakthrough, Creech has published more than twelve additional books for young readers. And in doing so, she has won even more acclaim and recognition. In 2001, her novel *The Wanderer* (2000) was named a Newbery Honor Book. In 2003, *Ruby Holler* (2002) won the United Kingdom's equivalent of the Newbery Medal—the Carnegie Medal. This gave Creech the distinction of being the first American ever to win the

8

Carnegie Medal, as well as being the first author in history to win both the Newbery and the Carnegie.

Creech continues to enchant readers and take them on journeys near and far. Many of her books are about literal quests. She strongly believes in the importance of being in beautiful surroundings, and Creech often takes her characters to places she has been. However, her books are also about the internal voyages of self-discovery with which her teenage protagonists are confronted.

When Creech studied literature in college, she learned that the inner voyages characters go on are as important as the outer ones. As she explains, "I am intrigued by the way the physical journeys (from this place to that place) mirror interior quests—how we are changed and shaped by where we go, who we meet, what we think along the way."[1] Reviewers acknowledge Creech's skill in combining external and internal journeys in her books. "Creech . . . demonstrates her expertise at evoking physical and emotional landscapes and the connections between the two,"[2] wrote a critic in the *Bulletin of the Center for Children's Books*.

Most of Creech's novels combine these journeys in a multilayered approach. While Creech's Newbery Honor book, *The Wanderer,* is an adventurous tale about a literal voyage (the dangerous journey of a sailboat across the Atlantic Ocean), it is also a touching story of the main protagonists as they come to accept, appreciate, and love each other. In Creech's Newbery Award–winning novel, *Walk Two Moons*, thirteen-year-old Salamanca's travels across the United States with her grandparents are mirrored by her internal adventure of coming to accept and understand why her mother has left her family.

In her Newbery Medal acceptance speech for *Walk Two Moons*, Creech told the audience that many of the ideas in the book (including the title) were inspired by a proverb she'd found in a fortune cookie. The fortune said, "Don't judge a man until you've walked two moons in his moccasins."[3] In part, the proverb appealed to her because she'd always seen stories as invitations in which characters might say,

> Come along and walk with us a while, slip into our moccasins so that you might see what we think and feel, and so that you might understand why we do what we do, and so that you might glimpse the larger world outside your own.[4]

Creech herself has always loved reading because of the way books allow her to live vicariously through the characters she encounters. She can become somebody else for a short time, and this is an experience she relishes—as do readers of her books. Her unique sensitivity toward appreciating and expressing new and vivid experiences, coupled with her ability to convincingly integrate this into her writing, is what makes her such a popular young adult author.

Not surprisingly, looking at the world from the points of view of her characters is one aspect that attracted Creech to writing. She takes joy in discovering and understanding what makes people different, even if others consider those differences odd. In her writing, Creech creates characters who are completely unique. In fact, many of them are slightly eccentric. These characters include Salamanca's imaginative friend Phoebe in *Walk Two Moons*, the loony but lovable Uncle Nate in *Chasing Redbird* (1997), and Tiller, Sairy, Dallas, and Florida in *Ruby Holler*. As book reviewer Joanna Brod wrote, "Creech's storytelling sorcery [magic] is matched only by her quirky yet down-to-earth characters."[5]

No matter how offbeat her protagonists, as she writes, Creech puts herself into their shoes and into their hearts. Writing from the perspective of her teenage characters, she remembers her own feelings, fears, and concerns during adolescence. She understands what a hard time teenage years can be. Her novels deal with true-to-life issues that all adolescents have to struggle with, such as building an identity, questioning relationships, and experiencing the pain of death and loss. As they work through their quests, Creech's protagonists are able to take control of their lives, thereby becoming hopeful, independent, and self-assured.

Just as in her own life, serious moments mix with funny ones in Sharon Creech's novels. She uses her clever sense of wit to make the serious and painful issues her protagonists face easier for readers to bear. "This comes out of who I am," Creech explains. "I cannot dwell too long in the serious before lightening the mood with humor."[6]

As with any adventure, it could be said that the best part is coming home again. Creech's home and family have always been the most important part of her life. From the relatives and friends she was close to while growing up, to her own husband and children, Creech is rooted to her family by a deep connection. Her books are similarly grounded in family relationships, from Gram and Gramps Hiddle, who travel with Salamanca in *Walk Two Moons*, to Mary Lou Finney's loud and crazy family in *Absolutely Normal Chaos* (1995). These very real and loving family ties make Creech's books special.

The characters she creates often have to come to terms with a change in their family situation.

For example, in *Walk Two Moons*, Salamanca must adjust to the loss of her mother. In *Ruby Holler*, Dallas and Florida get a brand-new family, and are not sure whether they can accept it. In Creech's recent book, *Heartbeat* (2004), Annie must come to terms with both a new baby in the family and the deterioration of her adored grandfather's health.

Sharon Creech's journeys have, in a sense, brought her home again, too. She has moved back to the United States from England and is now living in New Jersey. She and her husband still travel a lot, and Creech's zest for new people, places, and discoveries continues to shine through in the books she writes.

1 Starting Out with Stories

Sharon Creech was born on July 29, 1945, in Mayfield Heights, Ohio, a suburb of the city of Cleveland. She was the second-eldest of five children born to Ann and Arvel Creech. As the Creech family grew, it moved to bigger homes within the Cleveland area to accommodate its members. Sharon went to kindergarten at Shore Elementary in Euclid, right across the street from her house. After a move, she began first grade at Oxford Elementary School in Cleveland Heights. It was there that she learned how to read. Once she finished second grade, the Creeches moved to South Euclid, where they lived in a big two-story white house with black shutters. Sharon

14

would take a bus to Victory Park Elementary in South Euclid for the rest of her elementary school years and would live in the Buxton Road home until she graduated from high school.

With an older sister, Sandy, and three younger brothers, Dennis, Doug, and Tom, the Creech home was a happy, noisy place. Both of Sharon's parents worked, Arvel as an accountant and Ann as an office manager. Life seemed downright chaotic at times, and Sharon would later describe her early years as being filled with "absolutely normal chaos." As an adult, she would think back on this chaos, which she missed dearly, and write a fictional account of her family life called *Absolutely Normal Chaos*. The story, which was set in her home on Buxton Road, would become her very first book for young readers.

Sharon's childhood was also filled with relatives. She had a large extended family, with grandparents, aunts, uncles, and cousins. They would often get together and gather around the kitchen table. Then they would tell family tales, and each person would try to top the last. This was where Sharon first learned to tell stories. "Here I learned to exaggerate and embellish," she explains, "because if you didn't, your story was drowned out by someone else's more exciting one."[1] It was a skill she would never forget.

The Creech family often traveled to Quincy, Kentucky, to visit Sharon's cousins on a farm near the Ohio River. Sharon and her cousins spent their days running around on the hills surrounding the farm. They climbed trees, splashed in the swimming hole nearby, and played in the barn. Then, at night, everyone would gather on the porch, where more stories were told. Sharon loved the rural community of Quincy where everybody knew each other and life seemed isolated from the outside world. She would later use her cousins' farm and the town of Quincy as the setting for her novel *Chasing Redbird*. In the novel, she gave the town the fictional name of Bybanks. Bybanks was also mentioned in her novels *Walk Two Moons*, *Bloomability*, and *The Wanderer*.

Whether in Kentucky or at home in Ohio, Sharon loved to play outside. She spent much of her childhood riding her bike near her home, running around, and climbing trees or anything else she could find to climb. When she was not playing, she loved to read. "I don't remember the titles of books I read as a child," Sharon says, "but I do remember the experience of reading—of drifting into the pages and living in someone else's world, the excitement of never knowing what lay ahead." She continues, "I loved myths—American Indian myths, Greek myths, and the King Arthur legends—and I remember the lightning jolt of exhilaration when I read *Ivanhoe* [Sir Walter Scott, 1820] as a teenager. These were all magical worlds, full of mystery and imagination: anything could happen, anything at all."[2]

Sharon particularly liked Native American myths because her cousin had told her that one of the family's ancestors was a Native American. Her favorite myth was that of Estsanatlehi, a woman who didn't die when she grew old but instead turned into a baby again. In that way, she lived a thousand lives over and over again. Enamored with the idea that she was part Native American, Sharon used to exaggerate as a child and tell people that she was a full-blooded Native American. She would reenact the myths in the woods near her home, creeping around and playing out the stories.

When Sharon thought about getting older, there were many things she wanted to be when she grew up, including a painter, an ice skater, a singer, and a teacher. However, she would find that her skills in painting, ice skating, and singing were limited, so Sharon became a teacher. As a child, Sharon loved school, and the first day of school was her favorite day of the year. With fresh paper and new pens and pencils, Sharon began each school year with great excitement. Sharon was a very good student and even liked doing her homework. She enjoyed all of her classes and teachers, and remembers being particularly fond of her sixth grade teacher, Ms. Zolar, whom she mentions in her book *Absolutely Normal Chaos*. She would later say that the praise and encouragement she received from her teachers gave her the confidence that ultimately helped her become a writer.

When she was around eleven or twelve years old, Sharon began to develop a real interest in writing. One of her favorite things to do was to pretend she was a reporter. However, she decided it was no fun to stick to the facts. Instead, she made up outlandish stories about the people in her neighborhood. On rainy days, she would write funny poems and give them away as gifts to her family and friends. In the summer, she and her siblings made up plays that they would act out for their parents and neighbors. Despite her confidence with words, as a child Sharon was sometimes shy when she was not with her family or friends. She was much more of an observer. This was particularly apparent when the Creech family piled into the car for vacation every summer and went somewhere new. Sharon remembers studying the people they met, looking at the way they moved, and noting their accents as they spoke. "I wanted to memorize everything I saw and heard, because it was all so fascinating,"[3] she recalls. When Sharon was eleven, her family took a vacation to Idaho. She recalls the awe with which she watched the beautiful scenery out the window of the car. She celebrated her twelfth birthday on that trip, and when the family stopped at a Native American trading post, Sharon chose a pair of beaded moccasins as a present. The trip had such a powerful effect on Sharon that she would re-create it more than thirty years later when she wrote *Walk Two Moons*.

In junior high school, Sharon continued to become more quiet and reflective. Memorial Junior High was a large school, and Sharon felt uncomfortable around so many new students. However, it was at Memorial Junior High that Sharon met one of her lifelong friends, Linda Adams. Sharon and Linda talked on the phone every night, rode their bikes together, and ate chocolate ice cream every day during the summer.

At school, Sharon was an excellent student. In fact, each spring she was part of a group who received free tickets to a Cleveland Indians baseball game as a reward for getting good grades. Though Sharon wasn't particularly interested in baseball, she enjoyed these trips. She liked eating hot dogs in the ballpark and enjoyed having the chance to look at all the crazy baseball fans at the game.

High School

In high school, Sharon continued to enjoy her classes. She had a wonderful English teacher who got her excited about reading poetry. The rhythms, sounds, and feelings expressed in the poems made a lasting impression on her. After school, Sharon did not participate in extracurricular activities because she had to catch the bus home. She was not much of a "joiner" and sometimes felt socially lost during those difficult teenage years. Thinking back to this period in her life, she says, "As a teenager, I always thought that everyone else knew something that I didn't; that there must be a manual out there that I didn't have access to! I still feel that way some days."[4]

Sharon did enjoy some special responsibilities during school hours, such as being an office aide and a hall monitor. "Sounds kind of boring, but I liked those 'jobs,'"[5] Sharon recalls. At home, she also had many responsibilities. She and her sister, Sandy, were often put in charge of their three younger brothers. When Sandy went off to college, Sharon took on more of these jobs herself. For example, she read to her youngest brother and gave first aid for the many bumps and scrapes that her energetic brothers would get as they ran around.

2 Traveling Far

Sharon Creech graduated from Brush High School in South Euclid in 1963. Because her sister, Sandy, had attended Hiram College in Ohio, Creech decided to go there as well. She really enjoyed the small, beautiful campus. Because there were so many things Creech wanted to do with her life, it was hard for her to choose a single major. She wished she could try everything. As Creech recalls,

> I told a roommate that I wanted to try every job there was for three months at a time. It was all sorts of jobs I was interested in: writing, painting, house-building, tree-trimming, teaching, acting.[1]

Thinking she would become a teacher, Creech began college as an education major. However, she quickly realized that she liked her English classes best, so she switched her major to English literature.

It wasn't until her last year at Hiram that she took her first writing class. On the first day of class, the professor, a visiting British writer, gave Creech and her fellow students their assignment for the semester. They each had to write a novel. No other instructions were given, except that the first chapter was due in a week. Creech was shocked by the magnitude of the assignment. Even worse, she had no idea what to write. She spent the week in a trance, trying to come up with ideas.

Pretending to be the writers she'd seen in the movies, Creech sat in front of her typewriter, wrote, and then ripped out one piece of paper after another. She'd crumple them up and toss them dramatically to the floor. Finally, on the day before the first chapter was due, Creech decided that if she couldn't make up a fictional story, she'd write about something that had actually happened to her. She ended up writing about a trip she'd taken the previous summer, when she and her boyfriend had driven from Ohio to Mexico in an old, beat-up Volkswagen. She changed the names of the characters, invented some new details to make it more interesting, and handed it in.

When she got the chapter back, her professor had two comments. He thought the names she'd given her characters were boring, but he liked her first sentence, "Last summer we drove from Ohio to Mexico."[2] He said that it followed a classical, archetypal journey structure. However, it wouldn't be until she was in graduate school that Creech would understand what he meant. Although she never finished writing that novel, the class inspired her to dream of becoming a novelist. She thought about how wonderful it would be to make up new worlds and characters and write about them in books.

Creech's years in college fed her passions for reading and writing. She knew that she wanted to work with books in her life, either as a teacher or a writer. It would turn out that she'd do both. In 1967, Creech graduated from Hiram College with a bachelor of arts degree in English literature. That same year, Sharon and her boyfriend, H. R. Leuthy Jr., got married. During the next few years, they would have two children together. Their son, Robert, was born in 1968, and their daughter, Karin, was born in 1971.

Graduate School

Once her children were in school, Creech decided to continue her study of literature and writing in graduate school. She and her family had moved to the Washington, D.C., area, where her husband had gotten a job, and Creech found a program at nearby George Mason University, where she could attend classes at night. In graduate school, she studied literature in more depth and took classes and workshops in writing. She had the privilege of studying under many great writers who visited the school. Some of these visiting writers were only there for a quick workshop; others stayed longer.

One such writer was John Gardner, an acclaimed American novelist and teacher whose books include *The Wreckage of Agathon* (1970). It was during one of Gardner's classes that Creech once again heard about the archetypal journey structure. Gardner explained that there are two main structures in novels: the journey structure, in which the main character goes on a literal or internal quest; and the stranger comes to town structure, in which someone new enters the main character's life. After listening to Gardner, these concepts began to make sense to Creech. It was at this point that she realized that lives and stories revolve around where we go (the journey structure) and who we meet (the stranger comes to town structure)—whether it is in our minds or out in the world.

Through her studies, Creech learned a lot about the craft of writing and storytelling. She also studied and wrote poetry. In fact, a few of her poems were even published in journals. This experience gave Creech a taste of how it felt to be a published writer, a feeling she enjoyed. During her last two years of graduate school, Creech also followed another interest. Since her childhood days when she'd made up plays, she had dreamed of writing a play that would be performed in a theater. Luckily, from 1975 to 1977, she got a job as a researcher for the Federal Theater Project Archives. Creech enjoyed the work. She learned a lot about theater and nursed her longing to write a play someday.

Moving On

In 1977, Creech graduated from George Mason University with a master's degree in English literature and writing. She got a job as an editorial assistant at a news magazine called *Congressional Quarterly*. Here, she edited articles about politics and government. Though the job gave her good writing experience, she did not enjoy the work. After two years, Creech decided it was time for something new. She and her husband had divorced in 1977, and at this point, she was a single mother with two children. She was ready to change the direction of her life.

When a friend told Creech about an opportunity to move to England, she was interested. Her friend worked at a school called TASIS—The American School in Switzerland. The branch of the school in Surrey, England, was looking for an English teacher. Though Creech did not have a teaching degree (which prohibited her from teaching in public schools), she was qualified to teach at TASIS because it was a private school. Creech felt that her degrees in literature and writing qualified her to teach English. Taking this job would also mean that her children would receive a top-notch education at the school and have wonderful travel opportunities.

When the headmaster of TASIS came to the United States to meet with prospective teachers, Creech interviewed for the job. However, she didn't feel that it went well. The headmaster had expressed many concerns about whether she, as a single mother with two children, could handle all the demands of being a teacher. Creech, who thought that these were unfair concerns, was very upset and decided to fight for the job. She wrote the headmaster a long and impassioned letter, telling him exactly why she was the right person for the job. The letter must have worked, because Creech was hired. In the summer of 1979, she and her children moved to Surrey, England.

The Surrey TASIS branch was housed in a Georgian mansion surrounded by trees and gentle green hills. "I thought I'd landed in heaven,"[3] Creech recalls of her arrival in England. The country was beautiful. For most of her years there, she would live in the tiny village of Thorpe, in a small white house called the Walnut Tree Cottage. It was an old home, but well kept, with roses climbing up an out-side wall, and an apple tree in the backyard.

The demands on Creech as a new teacher were difficult. She remembers the chaotic days of preparation leading up to the first day of school when both of her children had the flu. However, Creech was determined to prove herself, and she worked hard to begin her new career as a teacher of American and British literature.

Shortly after she'd arrived, Creech was walking through the school's courtyard when she met a man named Lyle Rigg, who had just been hired as the assistant headmaster. It was a hot day and he offered her some ice, which was not as easy to find in England as it was in the United States. During their conversation, Creech discovered that Rigg was also from Ohio. He'd come to England after living in Boston and Brazil. Creech and Rigg developed a strong friendship and fell in love. Three years later, in 1982, they got married. They celebrated their wedding with a riverboat party on England's river Thames.

After their marriage, Lyle, Sharon, Rob, and Karin moved to Montagnola, Switzerland. The Swiss branch of TASIS had offered Lyle a position as its headmaster. There, in the beautiful foothills of the Alps, Creech taught English, the children attended school, and they all enjoyed the lovely scenery that surrounded them. After two years, Lyle was offered the headmaster's position at the English branch of TASIS and the family moved back to Surrey, England.

A Wonderful Teacher

Creech continued to pour all of her energy into her teaching career, and was known as a wonderful teacher. Fueled by her love for children and literature, she worked hard and expected her students to do the same. Because her son, Rob, had had trouble in school in Washington, D.C., Creech tried to become the teacher she wished he'd had. Instead of expecting her students' learning style to conform to the group (as Rob's teachers had done) she respected their different ways of learning and worked to develop their individual strengths. She encouraged students to think for themselves, and celebrated their unique opinions about the books, stories, and poetry she shared with them.

Though most of the students at TASIS were American, many were from other countries. Creech developed an appreciation for the way their cultures shaped who they were. Looking back, Creech feels that getting to know the diverse group of students at TASIS helped her as a writer. The variety of interpretations her students offered of the books they read showed Creech what her students connected with in their reading and helped her shape her own idea of a good story. Creech feels that many aspects of her teaching helped her as a novelist. "In many ways, teaching and traveling offered the perfect training ground for writing," she explains. "I had to study classical literature in order to teach it. Our students read Shakespeare and then traipse off to Stratford to clomp through his house. We read Chaucer's *Canterbury Tales* and then take the train down to Canterbury and follow in his pilgrims' steps. It all comes alive in this way."[4]

During this period, Creech's many responsibilities did not leave her time to work on the novels she'd always dreamed of writing. As the wife of the school's headmaster, Creech also hosted and attended school events with Lyle and helped with the many crises that arose at the school. Nonetheless, Creech still found time occasionally to write stories and poems for her children. Once they started high school, Creech began writing her own poetry again. For the first time since graduate school, she began to submit her poetry for publication in journals. Once a month, she sent out more poems. "Yes, they often were rejected," Creech recalls, "but I just kept sending them out. This was just part of the process—I expected 'acceptance' to take a while. Periodically one would be accepted! Wow!"[5]

3 The Words Begin to Pour

The story of Sharon Creech's beginning as a novelist goes back to just after she and her children moved to England. About nine months after they moved, Creech's father suffered a massive stroke. It left him paralyzed and unable to speak clearly or understand words. Creech went back to the United States as often as she could to be with him.

Six years later, in 1986, Creech's father died. Sharon mourned his death, and then, about a month after he'd passed away, she suddenly found herself feeling an irresistible urge to write. She began writing a story, which got longer and longer until she realized it was a novel. Though she was still juggling her many responsibilities, she somehow found time to write. She poured every bit of extra time and energy into her work and the words flowed from her. After her first novel was finished, she began another one. It wasn't until later that Creech would understand the reasons for her sudden urge to write after her father's death. "The connection between my father's death and my flood of writing might be that I had been confronted with the dark wall of mortality: we don't have endless time to follow our dreams," Creech explains, "but it might also be that I felt obligated to use the words that my father could not."[1] Her father had been unable to use words for six long years. After his death, Sharon felt a need to put those silenced words to use. She also knew that if she wanted to write novels, she'd better get started.

Along with the novels, Creech continued to write poetry. In 1988, she won a contest with a poem called "Cleansing." The Billee Murray Denny Poetry Award, sponsored by Lincoln College in Illinois, gave her a cash payment of $1,000. Creech felt encouraged by the award. She was beginning to realize that other people might be interested in what she wrote.

Publishing Novels

By this point, Creech had completed two novels. The first was called *The Recital*, an adult story

33

about an eccentric woman who lived in a small town. It was a serious story, and Creech had wanted to write something funny when she'd finished it.

Because she missed her family in the States and wanted to relive the closeness they had all felt when she was growing up, the second novel she wrote was a lighthearted story about a big, loud, crazy family. She called it *Absolutely Normal Chaos*.

During the time she was writing the novel, Creech was teaching her high school students about keeping journals. Because of this, she decided to write *Absolutely Normal Chaos* in journal form. The story is a fictionalized account of Creech's childhood in which the main character, thirteen-year-old Mary Lou Finney, writes in a journal about her summer. In the novel, Mary Lou has an older sister and three younger brothers, whom Creech named after her real brothers. Though many of the things that happen in the story did not really happen to Creech, the visit of Mary Lou's older cousin, Carl Ray, was based on the extended visit of Creech's cousin when she was Mary Lou's age. Carl Ray's quiet, quirky personality in the book is similar to that of Creech's cousin.

Wanting to publish her novels, Creech began searching for a literary agent who would submit her work to publishers. It wasn't long before she'd found an agent in London who liked her work and wanted to represent her. About nine months after she'd found the agent, Creech received a call from him telling her that her first novel, *The Recital*, had been accepted for publication. "I was ecstatic!" she remembers. "I felt relieved (all that work was not for nothing) and tremendously excited."[2] The publisher, a British company in London called Pan Macmillan, had not only accepted *The Recital* (1990), but it had also contracted Creech to write another adult novel. The next book she would write was called *Nickel Malley* (1991), a story about a man's relationship with his neighbors.

In her early years as a novelist, Creech also wrote a play called *The Centre of the Universe: Waiting for the Girl*, which would be performed in 1992, in an off-Broadway festival in New York City. She wrote another adult novel, too, which was 800 pages long. However, her agent had no luck finding a publisher for that novel. Ultimately, Creech, who felt badly about the rejections, decided to put the manuscript away. It still sits on her closet shelf, and it is Creech's only novel to date that has not been published.

Because her agent had given her more good news, Creech did not leave herself time to feel badly about the rejections. As it turned out, *Absolutely Normal Chaos* (1990) had also been accepted by Pan Macmillan. Because the story was written from the perspective of a teenager, Pan Macmillan wanted to publish it as a novel for young readers. Pan Macmillan liked her writing so much, the company asked Creech to write another book. As a teacher and a reader, Creech had been living in the world of adult literature for so long that she had not realized there was a separate field of children's literature. She knew if she was going to write children's books, she'd better find out more about them.

She researched the field of children's literature, read children's books, and attended a conference where she heard Newbery Medal–winning author Lois Lowry (*The Giver*, 1994) speak. As Lowry talked about the many aspects of writing books for children, Creech realized that she'd already been doing these things. She had enjoyed writing from a teenager's point of view when she'd written *Absolutely Normal Chaos*. Because she had such vivid recollections of her teenage years and since she was gaining so much from her teaching experience, Creech decided she was ready to write her next children's book.

Many Steps to Success

For her next effort, Creech wanted to write a sequel to *Absolutely Normal Chaos*, which had chronicled Mary Lou Finney's summer in a journal written as an English assignment. Creech continued Mary Lou's story and wrote about what would happen after she turned in the journal to her English teacher when the new school year started. Creech finished the new manuscript and gave it to her editor at Pan Macmillan. Unfortunately, however, she did not get a positive response. Her editor liked the manuscript but told Creech that the publishing industry was losing money and the new story wasn't strong enough to sell well. She asked Creech if she would be willing to expand the novel to make the story stronger.

Although Creech thought she'd done all she could with Mary Lou's tale, she was willing to revise the manuscript and try a different approach. She added a new character to the story—a friend of Mary Lou Finney's named Phoebe Winterbottom. Over the next year, Creech continued writing, with Phoebe's unique and imaginative voice narrating the story. She also added some new elements to the novel. These included the disappearance of Phoebe's mother and the introduction of a stranger in the neighborhood whom Phoebe is convinced is a lunatic. Once she was finished, Creech gave the manuscript to her publisher, only to be met once more with disappointment. Creech had been assigned another editor, and unfortunately, the new editor also felt that the story wasn't finished. Recalling her feelings of this time, Creech said that at that point, she "was ready to toss it into the trash."[3]

However, instead of giving in to defeat, she persevered and began to think about how she could improve the book. Ideas did not come easily, though, and eventually, she became frustrated. Then, one day, Creech was digging through her purse and she found a slip of paper. It was a fortune she'd received at a Chinese restaurant where she'd recently dined. The fortune read, "Don't judge a man until you've walked two moons in his moccasins."[4] Creech had thought it was odd to have a Native American proverb in a Chinese fortune cookie.

The proverb sparked memories of her childhood. It made her think of journeys, and she remembered the family vacation she'd taken from Ohio to Idaho, and when she'd been given beautiful beaded moccasins at the Native American trading post. She also remembered how she'd been fascinated by what her cousin had said about their family sharing Native American heritage. Creech was eager to find out more about this mysterious part of her background. Somehow, she wanted to use these things she'd been reminded of in her story, but she was not sure how.

Walk Two Moons

On the days that she wasn't teaching, Creech had become accustomed to writing for most of the morning. She found that in the afternoon, her brain was too muddled to keep working, so she often took a nap. She would call these naps research naps or inspiration naps. Upon waking up an hour or so later, her thinking would have cleared and she could find a new way of approaching a frustrating part of the narrative she was working on. One day, soon after finding the fortune in her purse, Creech was still frustrated with the story of Phoebe and Mary Lou Finney, and she decided to take a nap.

When she woke up, a line of dialogue was floating in her head: "Gramps says that I'm a country girl at heart, and that is true."[5] The character who was speaking was not Phoebe or Mary Lou Finney, but someone new. Creech took clues from the line to learn about this new character. It seemed to

Creech that the girls' grandpa was important to her, and so was her background as a country girl. Creech also thought that the girl was thoughtful and gentle. The other information that Creech sensed was that this girl was going on a journey.

Creech began writing a third version of the book, starting with the line in her head as the opening sentence. She also decided that this new character would be the narrator. Since college, Creech made a special effort to find interesting names for her protagonists. She wanted the names to evoke their personalities or backgrounds. For this new character, Creech found a name on a map of New York: Salamanca. The character's full name became Salamanca Tree Hiddle. It sounded Native American, which led Creech to believe that this person would be partially Native American. And just as Creech had been when growing up, the character would be curious about her roots.

"I didn't have the vaguest idea what her story was when I began," Creech says. "I just liked her voice, and I followed her along. Each day, when I'd re-read the story from the beginning, I'd pick up a new 'clue,' and then I'd follow that thread."[6] Creech has found that she often writes this way. She doesn't plan stories out ahead of time, but simply starts working and sees where the writing takes her.

She enjoys the excitement of discovery as a new plot unfolds.

Salamanca's tale is about a journey—the same journey Creech had taken across the United States to Lewiston, Idaho, when she was twelve. Looking back, Creech wonders if she chose to do this because she missed her family in the United States. In addition, Creech's daughter, Karin, had gone back to the United States for college. Creech thinks that she may have transferred her sense of loss and emptiness to Salamanca, who desperately misses her mother.

Creech combined Sal's tale with the stories of Phoebe and Mary Lou, which she'd written before. She later joked that she was just too stubborn to throw away these earlier drafts of the novel. Creech wove the three stories together so that all of the characters and their individual journeys worked together. After many drafts, they became a tightly woven novel. She titled the book *Walk Two Moons*.

The plot of the story follows Salamanca's journey with Gram and Gramps Hiddle across the United States to Idaho, where Salamanca's mother had gone when she left the family. During the trip, Sal tells Gram and Gramps the story of how she and her friend Phoebe had to work through Phoebe's family problems. Sal flashes back

41

occasionally to memories of her mother, and slowly, as the journey continues, the stories all come together.

The trip itself has its moments of joy and sorrow, and Sal, Gram, and Gramps come to rely on each other for support, encouragement, and love. The camaraderie of their interactions is touching and unique, as shown in this excerpt from the novel when Gram, Gramps, and Sal stop in Wyoming to see the geyser Old Faithful erupt:

> "It looks like an upsidey-down waterfall!" Gram said. All the while there was a walloping hissing, and I could have sworn the ground rumbled and trembled underneath us. A warm mist blew toward us and people started backing away.
>
> All except Gram. She stood there grinning, tilting her face up to the mist, and staring at that fountain of water. "Oh," she said. "Oh, huzza, huzza!" She shouted it into the air and noise . . .
>
> Gradually, Old Faithful slowed down. We watched it undo itself and retreat into its hole. We stood there even after everyone else had drifted away. At last Gram sighed and said, "Okay, let's go."
>
> We were inside the car and about to leave when Gram started to cry. "Gol-dang," Gramps said. "What's the matter?"

Gram sniffled. "Oh nothing. I'm so happy I got to see Old Faithful."

"You old gooseberry," Gramps said, and on we went. "We're gonna eat up Montana," Gramps said. "We're gonna get to the I-dee-ho border tonight. You watch me. I'm putting this pedal to the metal." He stepped on the gas and peeled out of the parking lot. "I-dee-ho, here we come."[7]

It took Creech a total of three years and eleven revisions before the book was finished. *Walk Two Moons* was accepted for publication by Macmillan Publishers in England and HarperCollins in the United States. To polish the story, Creech worked with editors at both companies. Interestingly, the British version of the novel and the American one ended up being slightly different. In fact, Creech recalls that working with two different publishers on the same story was quite challenging. To further complicate matters, at HarperCollins, three of her editors left the company before the book was finished. Finally, Creech was introduced to a fourth editor named Joanna Cotler. Cotler and Creech worked so well together that Cotler has edited all of Creech's books ever since.

When *Walk Two Moons* came out in 1994, it received mixed reviews. A writer in the *Kirkus Reviews* journal stated,

Creech, an American who has published novels in Britain, fashions characters with humor and sensitivity, but Sal's poignant story would have been stronger without quite so many remarkable coincidences or such a tidy sum of epiphanies at the end. Still, its revelations make it a fine yarn.[8]

Creech's storytelling ability, writing style, and characters were praised by reviewers, but some felt that the plot was too contrived, or unbelievable. Meanwhile, others called it too realistic because it forced readers to face such difficult issues as dysfunctional family life and death.

There were also some reviewers and Native American advocates who criticized the book because Sal's character was of Native American heritage and Creech is not a full-blooded Native American. They believed Creech was not qualified to write Sal's story. Many people came to Creech's defense, including children's literature critic and author Hazel Rochman, who wrote in the *New York Times Book Review* that "The Indianness is one of the best things about this book . . . For once in a children's book, Indians are people, not reverential figures in a museum diorama. Sal's Indian heritage is a natural part of her finding herself in America."[9]

44

The Newbery Medal

Creech was taken completely by surprise when she got the call telling her that *Walk Two Moons* had won the 1995 Newbery Medal. At the time, she'd been working on her next novel, *Chasing Redbird*. She was having such trouble with the ending that she'd literally stepped out into her backyard to scream. When the phone rang, she began to take a message, thinking the call would be for the headmaster about a crisis at the school. Creech was then shocked when she found out that the caller was Newbery Committee member Kathleen Horning. Horning was calling from Philadelphia, where the American Library Association (ALA) was having its midwinter convention. The Newbery Committee had just announced the 1995 medal winner, and Creech's *Walk Two Moons* had won. "Are you kidding?"[10] Creech asked Horning again and again. Even after she'd hung up and the entire Newbery Committee had shouted Gram's favorite phrase, "Huzza, huzza," over the phone, Creech still couldn't believe it.

During the following days, the phone rang off the hook. People were requesting interviews and information, and each time, Creech expected it would be the committee calling back saying they'd made a mistake. Creech knew so little about the world of children's books in the United States that when a representative from her publisher called shortly after she'd won the award, Creech asked her how many Newbery Medals were given each year. She didn't expect the answer she got: "One, Sharon. One."[11]

On Valentine's Day the following week, Sharon received a call from Lyle. During all of the excitement, he'd been gone on a two-week trip to the United States to interview prospective teachers for TASIS. Before he left, he'd hidden a Valentine's Day present in his sock drawer, and during his call he told Sharon to look for it. Sharon opened the present and began to cry. It was a miniature enameled egg, painted with pictures showing the phases of the moon, and around the top were the words, "May all your dreams come true."[12]

"I'll be honest: I never dreamed a dream this big,"[13] Creech confessed in her Newbery Medal acceptance speech later that year. The enormousness of the award she'd won had taken a while to sink in, but Creech would later say that it truly changed her life. As a result, she received invitations to travel to schools and conferences all over the world and meet thousands of readers, librarians, and teachers. Creech became so busy, in fact, that she had to take a leave of absence from teaching. Unfortunately, she never made it back to teaching, but she did move forward in great strides on her path as a novelist.

The Next Steps

After the success of *Walk Two Moons*, Harper-Collins decided to publish *Absolutely Normal Chaos*, which had been published in England in 1990. The U.S. release of *Absolutely Normal Chaos* was in 1995. The book received a warm welcome from readers and reviewers who knew Sharon Creech's name and were eager to read more of her work.

The next book Creech published was for young readers. *Pleasing the Ghost* (1996) was a chapter book about a nine-year-old boy named Dennis, whose Uncle Arvie (named after Creech's father) comes back to visit him in the form of a ghost. Inspired by the sad yet humorous way Creech's father had spoken after his stroke, Uncle Arvie tries to ask for Dennis's help in this lighthearted look at loss and love.

When she'd won the Newbery Medal, Creech had almost finished writing *Chasing Redbird*. She'd put it aside, spent three months writing her Newbery acceptance speech, and finally finished it. *Chasing Redbird*, published in 1997, tells the story of Zinny, a thirteen-year-old girl whose big family lives in a home near Bybanks, Kentucky. Creech had wanted to write more about Bybanks after finishing *Walk Two Moons*. She subtly connected the two stories by mentioning that Zinny and Salamanca had been friends. In *Chasing Redbird*, Zinny's aunt dies, and Zinny feels confused and thinks her aunt's death may somehow have been her fault. Overwhelmed by her feelings, Zinny retreats into the woods and meadows behind her home. She finds an old trail there and decides to uncover it. As she works to clear the twenty-mile-long (thirty-two-kilometer-long) trail, Zinny is able to resolve many issues that have been bothering her. Creech magically weaves together Zinny's external journey as she clears the trail, her internal voyage of self-discovery, and a humorous story line about a male friend who goes to great lengths to impress Zinny. Creech also includes a host of quirky family members, such as Zinny's loony uncle Nate who runs around trying to catch his departed wife, whom he calls his Redbird.

Chasing Redbird received positive reviews, including one from Ethel Heins of the *Horn Book Magazine* stating, "Creech has written a striking novel, notable for its emotional honesty."[14]

4 The Return Trip

In 1998, after living overseas for almost twenty years, Sharon and Lyle moved back to the United States. Their children were living in the States and the couple wanted to be closer to their family. During the previous year, Creech's mother had died, and Creech felt she had spent too much time traveling back and forth from England to the United States.

Back in the United States, Lyle began to look for a job. When he was offered a position as the headmaster of the Pennington School, a boarding and day school in Pennington, New Jersey, the two of them moved into a three-story, red-brick home on the school campus.

49

Bloomability

During the year before her move, Creech began to think about everything she would miss about Europe when she was gone. She loved England and was especially fond of Switzerland with its beautiful mountains and friendly people.

To keep her memories of Switzerland fresh in her mind, Creech decided to set a novel there. The book she wrote was the story of a thirteen-year-old girl who was born in Bybanks, Kentucky. Domenica Santolina Doone (called Dinnie for short) had moved from one state to another as her unstable father searched for work. When life finally became too complex, Dinnie's aunt Sandy and uncle Max took her with them to Switzerland to attend the boarding school where her uncle Max had been hired as headmaster. Creech based the school on the one where she'd taught for two years when her family lived in Switzerland.

The novel focuses on Dinnie's struggle to make friends with the diverse group of students at school. As the story progresses, she discovers her ability to embrace new opportunities instead of being scared of them. Creech provides vivid descriptions of the breathtaking mountain scenery as Dinnie begins to travel around Switzerland and learns how to ski. About midway through writing the novel, Creech treated herself to a trip to Switzerland to research the setting and confirm some of the details in her story. Creech also set an unusual goal when she wrote this novel: none of her characters would die. In all of her other children's books, at least one character dies. Happily, she met her goal.

Creech called the novel *Bloomability*. The word is coined by a foreign student in the novel who, because he is unable to correctly pronounce the word "possibility," instead says "bloomability." *Bloomability* was published in 1998, the year Sharon and Lyle moved back to the United States. Reviews of the book were positive. For example, a reviewer in *Booklist* wrote that it is "a story to stimulate both the head and heart."[1]

The Wanderer

When Creech began to think about her next book, she already had a strong feel for what the story would be about. It would mirror another journey, not one that Creech had taken, but one that her daughter, Karin, had taken. After Karin graduated from college, she decided to accompany six male friends on a voyage across the Atlantic Ocean from Connecticut to Ireland on a forty-five-foot (fourteen-meter) sailboat. Creech had been hesitant about this, but Karin assured her mother that her friends would take care of her. During the voyage, Karin kept a journal of everything that happened. This included a big storm halfway through their trip, during which a huge gale ripped their sails, damaged the boat, and ruined their communications equipment. Once they'd reached Ireland, Karin called her mother and told her that they had almost died.

After Creech recovered from the shock of this news, she realized that the voyage would make a great basis for a story. She began writing about a gutsy thirteen-year-old girl named Sophie, who decides to accompany her three uncles and two cousins on a journey across the ocean in their sailboat named the *Wanderer*. They are traveling to England to visit Sophie's uncles' father.

The story of the voyage is told through journal entries made on the trip by both Sophie and her thirteen-year-old cousin, Cody. Creech liked the idea of narrating the story from two different points of view. She also included Cody as a main character because of the many requests she had received from male readers who wanted her to write a book featuring a young male as a main protagonist. As the plot unfolded through the journals of Sophie and Cody, Creech came to realize many things about their personalities; for example, their secrets and fears, and what they each wanted most. She developed the framing story of the voyage and paralleled that journey with the inner self-discovery of her characters as they confronted their concerns and learned to get along with each other.

As she wrote, Creech drew from many different aspects of her life. The voyage of the *Wanderer* followed the same route Creech's daughter, Karin, had navigated on her trip across the ocean. And not surprisingly, the crew encountered a big storm that almost killed everybody on board. In the book, Creech also made use of two of her father's childhood stories and gave Sophie's grandfather the same cottage in Thorpe, England, in which she and her family had lived. In the following excerpt from the novel, Sophie describes the cottage and her reunion with her grandfather, Bompie, a nickname Creech's sister-in-law had given her grandfather when she was young.

Oh, Bompie!

I can see why he wanted to come home to his England. It's so pretty here, with roses climbing up the side of the house, and lavender spreading in big clumps along the walk, and inside are tiny rooms and wee windows and miniature fireplaces.

I had so wanted to see him alone, but instead we all clumped into the room together.[2]

The Wanderer was published in 2000. A highly coveted starred review in *Publishers Weekly* gave the novel tremendous praise. The review stated that "Like *Walk Two Moons*, this intimate novel poetically connects journey with self-discovery. Creech once again captures the ebb and flow of a vulnerable teen's emotional life, in this enticing [inviting] blend of adventure and reflection."[3] In 2001, Creech received the wonderful news that *The Wanderer* had been named a Newbery Honor Book and awarded the Christopher Award.

Love That Dog

As had happened with *The Wanderer*, the idea for Creech's next novel occurred many years before she began the book. However, this time, she didn't realize that the inspiration would lead to her writing a book. Years earlier, Creech had become friends with Kathleen Horning—the Newbery Committee member who called to let her know that she had won for *Walk Two Moons*. One year, Horning sent Creech a card on which the first stanza of a poem called "Love That Boy" was written. Popular young adult author and poet Walter Dean Myers had written the poem. Creech loved the energy, rhythm, and emotional strength Myers conveyed in the poem. She cut it out, posted it on the bulletin board near her desk, and read it many times a day. Then, one day, Creech began to think about the boy in the poem. It was obvious that the boy was loved, but what or who did he love? A dog, maybe, or a teacher? In response to these questions that she was asking herself, a character emerged in Creech's mind who loved both a dog and a teacher. And because Creech's inspiration was a poem, she sensed that her character Jack's story would also involve poetry.

In *Love That Dog*, the novel that grew from this inspiration, Creech's narrative revolves around journal entries Jack writes as his teacher, Mrs. Stretchberry, introduces poetry to her class. Like many of the students Creech remembered teaching, and as she herself had sometimes felt as a child, Jack thought poetry was stupid. Nonetheless, Mrs. Stretchberry persists in sharing poetry with her class. As a result of her efforts, Jack slowly comes around. When he reads a poem by Walter Dean Myers called "Love That Boy," he tries to create his own version of the poem, which he calls "Love That Dog." In it, he expresses his feelings about his beloved dog who has recently been hit by a car and killed. Jack decides to write a letter to Mr. Myers asking if he might come and visit his school. To his astonishment and delight, Myers agrees to visit.

This book, which Creech wrote in free verse, came to her more quickly and easily than any of her other books. In fact, she finished the book three months after she started writing. However, there was a problem. Though she had not expected the character of Walter Dean Myers to enter her story, he'd become quite an important part of it. As a result, Creech was worried about using a live poet and author as a character in a book. She didn't think it could be done. Because of her uncertainty, Creech hid the story in a drawer for several months.

When her editor, Joanna Cotler, asked her what she was working on, Creech told her she couldn't send her the story. Ultimately, Cotler persuaded Creech to let her take a look at the manuscript, and she loved it. In response to Creech's dilemma, Cotler suggested they send the manuscript to Walter Dean Myers to see what he thought about being included in the book. This idea made Creech very nervous. She'd only met Myers once at a conference. She decided that if he had any reservations about being in the book, she'd forget about the whole thing. However, as it turned out, Walter Dean Myers liked the idea.

After *Love That Dog* was published in 2001, it ended up winning the 2001 Christopher Award and receiving rave reviews. "Not only has she [Creech] shown young readers what a poem can do," wrote Meg Wolitzer in the *New York Times Book Review,* but "she's also shown them what a novel can do."[4]

Eager to branch out and try new things with her writing, Creech had begun writing picture books. Her first, *Fishing in the Air* (2000), is a lyrical piece based on a memory she had of fishing with her father and the power of imagination as she visualized the home where he'd grown up. The second book, *A Fine, Fine School* (2001), is a funny take on Creech's present life. She sometimes questions whether her husband, Lyle, becomes too enthusiastic about scheduling additional school activities for his students. The result of this is Creech's hilarious picture book about a lovable school principal who adds too much school to his students' lives.

Ruby Holler

A memory about Creech's father was the inspiration for Creech's next novel. Several years earlier, Creech had received a letter from her father's sister. The letter described his mischievous exploits with his siblings when he was young. Her aunt's story ended with the line, "and that was when we lived in the holler" [a hollow; a small valley between mountains].[5] Creech, who hadn't known that her father had lived in a holler, was very intrigued. She wondered what this place was like. Soon enough, she began to imagine a beautiful holler, and it was here that she envisioned her grandparents' home surrounded by hills and trees. Creech thought this would be a great location to set a story.

Even though she had the setting figured out, it took Creech several years to figure out who the characters in her story would be. She has said that in order to begin a book, she needs to have a clear image of her protagonists and her setting. Eventually, she came up with two very mischievous characters, thirteen-year-old orphans named Dallas and Florida. The twins, who have a reputation as troublemakers, are frequently whooped in their orphanage. Luckily, Dallas and Florida are invited by an older couple to live with them temporarily in their home in Ruby Holler. Though Dallas and Florida expect to be mistreated by Tiller and Sairy, the older couple actually turn out to be kind and nurturing. They want Dallas and Florida's help in getting ready for big adventures they're planning. The adventures don't exactly come off as Tiller and Sairy had hoped, but ultimately, all four characters learn about themselves and become a close family.

It took Creech about six months to write the first draft of *Ruby Holler,* and then another year to revise it. She lost time when she had to throw out big sections of the book. She'd planned to set Sairy's big adventure in China, and Tiller's on the Mississippi River, and she spent about three months researching those places. However, once she'd finished writing, she realized that those sections of the book didn't fit with the narrative as a whole. Creech took them out and in their place, she made up imaginary destinations—the island of Kangadoon for Sairy's adventure, and the Rutabago River for Tiller's.

Many of Creech's previous books, including *Walk Two Moons, Bloomability,* and *The Wanderer* included real places in their settings. However, Creech realized that she preferred to write about imaginary destinations. She began to feel that the story would flow more freely when it was not weighed down with realism.

Although, at times, Creech became frustrated with the long revisions she went through in the writing process for *Ruby Holler,* she says that she generally enjoys revising because that's when new ideas come to her. As Creech explains, "A couple of my favorite chapters [in *Ruby Holler*] came to me late in the revision process—probably at the stage of fourth or fifth drafts." She continues, "It always amazes me that whole scenes can emerge after you think you might be finished with a book!"[6] *Ruby Holler* was published in 2002. In general, the novel received positive reviews; however, not all were glowing. The *Booklist* review called the novel "A stylized [not natural or spontaneous] yet solid story . . ."[7] Because of this, Creech was absolutely speechless when she heard the following announcement: *Ruby Holler* had been awarded the 2002 Carnegie Medal, the United Kingdom's equivalent of the Newbery Medal. "*Ruby Holler* is a deserving winner," stated Anne Marley, chair of the judges for the 2002 Carnegie Medal. "Sharon Creech is a great story-teller and *Ruby Holler* exemplifies this. It is a very gentle tale of love and self-discovery told with great subtlety, humour and lightness of touch."[8]

5 Home, Sweet Home

L ike those who have returned from a long voyage, Sharon Creech takes great pleasure in the comforts of home. She and Lyle still live in their red-brick home in Pennington, New Jersey, where they are surrounded by a bustling school campus. Creech travels a lot, and many of her journeys take her far away. However, Creech's next two novels take place very close to home, as well as close to the heart.

When Creech received the exciting news that her daughter was expecting her first child, she began thinking about becoming a grandmother. Thoughts of her grandparents—especially her

Italian maternal grandmother with whom she was closest—filled her mind. She pictured the many hours they'd spent together chatting and preparing meals in the kitchen, and she realized how much she had learned from her grandmother.

Creech's 2003 novel, *Granny Torrelli Makes Soup*, takes place primarily in a kitchen. The book is peopled with characters who rarely stray farther than the house next door. In the kitchen, though, twelve-year-old Rosie travels far emotionally as she listens to Granny Torrelli share wisdom and stories about her childhood in Italy. Rosie learns things about her grandmother and eventually discovers that she, too, has the capacity for friendship, forgiveness, and love. Rosie and her best friend, Bailey, are changed by what they've learned from Granny Torrelli. When their journey is over, they have grown and matured, and their friendship is stronger than ever.

The book was warmly received by readers and reviewers. A reviewer in *Publishers Weekly* commented, "Creech once again shows her ability to crystallize characters and express their emotions through very few, carefully chosen words. Her subtle [delicate, quiet] approach only enhances the novel's cumulative impact."[1]

Heartbeat

In her 2004 novel, *Heartbeat*, Creech continues to explore the theme of grandchild-grandparent relationships. However, this time, she does so in free-verse form. Creech was inspired by Karen Hesse's Newbery-winning novel, *Out of the Dust*, which also was written in free verse. In the novel, Creech, who is now a grandmother, explores a girl's relationship with her grandfather and the wonder of birth.

Creech explains her thoughts from when she was working on this novel:

> As I was writing this book, I felt as if I were taking the pulse of this young girl, Annie, who is trying to place herself on this spectrum [range] of life. Where does she fit in? She wonders what it would be like to be old, and what it would be like to be an infant, and how she became who she is, and who exactly is she, and why is she here? These are questions I had when I was Annie's age, when my grandparents were aging, and when my mother was expecting my youngest brother. I felt as if I were balancing on the cusp of some important life thread, and it was essential to try to understand where I was, in the larger scheme of things.[2]

The result is the lyrical story of a twelve-year-old girl. Annie, who loves the feel of her bare feet thumping on the grass as she runs, can't run away from the scary changes happening in her life. For example, her friend Max joins the track team and is running for all the wrong reasons, her beloved grandfather is becoming increasingly forgetful, and there is an alien baby growing inside her mother. A starred review in *Publishers Weekly* journal called *Heartbeat* an "insightful exploration of life's beginning and ending and the joys to be encountered on the journey."[3]

Still Going Strong

As she'd done with Annie in *Heartbeat*, Creech fully immerses herself in her protagonists when she writes. She believes that her readers have gotten to know her pretty well if they've met all the individuals who grace the pages of her books. As she explains, different parts of her personality come through in each character. For example, her vulnerable, questioning side is written into the character of Annie; her dramatic, emotional side takes the form of *Absolutely Normal Chaos*'s Mary Lou Finney; and her contemplative, poetic side is a part of Salamanca from *Walk Two Moons*.

Creech is surrounded with reminders of her previous books and the characters she has written about. Her bright, sunny office is decorated with sketches and artwork for her picture books, letters from readers, and gifts (lots of replica moons) from readers, family, and friends. The third-floor hallway leading to her office is filled with photos of family and friends, which she looks at often. On the bulletin board closest to her desk, Creech has hung her two favorite photos—each of her children on a mountain peak, looking as if they're on top of the world.

Creech writes using a gray iMac computer. When other commitments don't get in the way, she follows a daily schedule starting with work beginning at 8:30 AM. First, she reads and responds to e-mail for about an hour. Then she writes until about 12:30 PM, takes a lunch break, a walk, and then maybe a nap. For the rest of the afternoon, she continues writing, takes a break for dinner, and then gets back to work. Her workday ends at around 8:30 PM.

A good part of Creech's day is spent reading and revising what she's already written. When she gets stuck—if she can't resolve how to advance the plot, or figure out how to get a character out of a certain situation, for example—she walks around and around the small lake behind her house until she solves the problem. Often, when Creech is writing a book, her concentration is so intense that she thinks about the story all the time—even when she is not writing it. Creech says this is when she is likely to put her keys in the microwave or the phone in the refrigerator by accident.

After the first draft is complete, Creech lets it sit for a few weeks and then revises until she feels it's as good as it can be. She's always a bit nervous when she sends a new manuscript to her editor. She worries that Joanna Cotler will hate it and tell her to put it in the trash. Luckily, this hasn't happened. Cotler usually offers suggestions for changes and sometimes, while going over revisions, the two talk on the phone for hours. Creech often goes through a total of four or five drafts until she and Cotler feel that the novel is ready for publication. One of the things Creech likes best about her job is when the published book comes in the mail. She reads it again and sometimes wonders how she even managed to put together all of these words and ideas.

Creech continues to juggle the many responsibilities that come with her busy life. As the headmaster's wife, she helps organize school events. As a well-known, much-loved author, she travels all over the world to attend speaking engagements. A lot of her time is also spent writing speeches for presentations. Creech admits that she likes to give speeches but has a hard time writing them. Creech also receives many letters from readers. She says this is much like receiving birthday cards every day. Some weeks, she spends a whole day reading and answering her mail, trying to personally respond to as many letters as she can.

Though she works a lot, Creech still makes time for other things that are important to her. Her number-one priority is her family. In the summer, Sharon and Lyle spend precious (though sometimes chaotic) time with their children, their families, and their extended family, at a cottage they own at Chautauqua Lake in upstate New York.

While she's at the lake, Creech likes to canoe, kayak, swim, or lie in a hammock and read. Her tastes in books include adult and children's literature, and she tends to like realistic stories that combine both funny and serious elements—much like the books she writes. Some of her favorite children's books include Karen Hesse's *Out of the Dust* (1997) and *Witness* (2001), Jerry Spinelli's *Loser* (2002) and *Maniac McGee* (1990), and Christopher Paul Curtis's *The Watsons Go to Birmingham—1963* (1995). She enjoys reading year-round, as well as going to the theater, browsing in bookstores, taking walks, and going cross-country skiing in the winter.

As a writer, Sharon Creech is still going strong. She publishes at least one new book each year, and starts to write a new story each fall as the activity of a new school year begins around her. She has written and published many award-winning middle grade and young adult novels, along with poetry, a play, two books for adults, a chapter book, and several picture books. She wrote her newest picture book, *A Baby in a Basket: New Baby Songs* (2004), just after her granddaughter, Pearl, was born.

"I love the whole process of writing," Creech tells her readers, "from starting with a blank page, to watching scenes take place, to being swept up in another world!"[4] Readers look forward to her new books, and wonder what great things to expect next from this creative and prolific author who they've come to love.

Interview with
Sharon Creech

ALICE B. MCGINTY: What have been some of your favorite moments as an author?

SHARON CREECH: I've had many, many favorite moments. Some of these include:

- visiting a group of students called The Basketball Poets in Supply, North Carolina, who, under the direction of an enthusiastic coach/teacher, combine the reading of poetry with the playing of basketball! They recited portions of *Love That Dog* for me;
- receiving a beautiful, heartfelt video from a class in Indianapolis;
- seeing a child in an airport curled up with one of my books;

- doing impromptu readers' theater with students across the country;
- and receiving that glorious Newbery Medal.

ALICE B. MCGINTY: What do readers say they like most about your books?

SHARON CREECH: It varies. Perhaps most often they say that they felt as if they were "in the book," that they were the character. Others love the humor, while some love the more poignant bits; nearly all love particular characters with whom they identify.

ALICE B. MCGINTY: Why do you feel you've been so successful as an author?

SHARON CREECH: That's very hard for me to say. I hope it's because I've worked hard and, as a result, I hope the books are well-written and thoughtful, and that they combine humor with seriousness.

ALICE B. MCGINTY: In which areas would you like to see yourself grow as a writer?

SHARON CREECH: I'd like to continue to try new forms and to continue to have at least one new technical challenge in each book.

ALICE B. MCGINTY: What is your relationship with your editor like?

SHARON CREECH: Our relationship has evolved over the course of many books. Ours is, I think, an honest and open relationship. She is supportive of my efforts and open to new ideas and offers thoughtful suggestions. I appreciate her time and her wisdom and pay close attention to each comment. We might not always agree, but it feels fine to disagree.

ALICE B. MCGINTY: Do you read reviews of your books? How do positive or negative reviews of your books affect you?

SHARON CREECH: If reviews are passed on to me by my publisher, I read them, but otherwise I don't seek them out. Naturally, positive and glowing reviews feel wonderful. I am grateful when a reviewer has done a thoughtful reading and offers intelligent comments. I can't recall any completely negative reviews, but some have included the occasional "snarky" comment, with which I usually disagree silently. Sometimes these snarky comments reveal more about the reviewer than about the book.

ALICE B. MCGINTY: Your soon-to-be published novel is called *Replay*. I've been told that it is a play within a play. Could you tell us a bit about the inspiration behind the book?

SHARON CREECH: It's more a novel with a play attached. It's primarily the story of a boy and his father. The boy "replays" events in his imagination, giving them a more favorable light. He is also in a play at school, and elements of the play parallel his growing understanding of himself and his father. At the end of the book, the play (supposedly written by his teacher) is included.

I've long been interested in theater and liked the idea of writing about a character interested in drama. That's how the story began, with that notion.

ALICE B. MCGINTY: You've written books for adults, young adult novels, middle grade novels, a chapter book, picture books, and a play. Are there any other genres of writing you'd like to try?

SHARON CREECH: Probably, but I can't think what they'd be at the moment. Right now I'm happy to continue writing in the above genres.

ALICE B. MCGINTY: Traveling to beautiful places has been very important to you in your life. What is the most beautiful place you've ever seen? Could you briefly describe it?

SHARON CREECH: There isn't just one place—there are many—and these include the Badlands, rugged Idaho, the rocky shores of the west and east coasts of America, the Alps in Switzerland, and the moors of northern England and Scotland. What these places have in common are vast, open, dramatic vistas, where the eye sees only the natural beauty of the earth. Spectacular.

ALICE B. MCGINTY: Are you planning any new journeys or adventures in the future?

SHARON CREECH: These days I prefer to stay home and take my journeys and adventures in the books I write.

Timeline

1945 Sharon Creech is born on July 29, in Mayfield Heights, Ohio.
1963 Creech graduates from Brush High School in South Euclid, Ohio.
1967 Creech graduates from Hiram College, in Hiram, Ohio, with a bachelor's degree in English literature. Creech marries H. R. Leuthy.
1968 Creech's son, Rob, is born.
1971 Creech's daughter, Karin, is born.
1973 Creech and her family move to Washington, D.C.
1977 Creech graduates from George Mason University in Fairfax, Virginia, with a master's degree in English literature and writing. Creech and H. R. Leuthy divorce.

1979 Creech accepts a position as an English teacher for TASIS in Surrey, England, and moves to England with her two children.

1982 Creech marries Lyle Rigg. Creech, Rigg, Rob, and Karin move to Montagnola, Switzerland.

1984 The family moves back to Surrey, England.

1988 Creech receives the Billee Murray Denny Poetry Award for her poem "Cleansing."

1990 *The Recital* is published in Great Britain.

1990 *Absolutely Normal Chaos* is published in Great Britain.

1991 *Nickel Malley* is published in Great Britain.

1994 *Walk Two Moons* is published in Great Britain and the United States.

1995 *Walk Two Moons* wins the Newbery Medal.

1995 *Absolutely Normal Chaos* is published in the United States.

1996 *Pleasing the Ghost* is published.

1997 *Chasing Redbird* is published.

1998 Creech and Rigg move from England to Pennington, New Jersey.

1998 *Bloomability* is published.

2000 *The Wanderer* is published.

2000 *Fishing in the Air* is published.

2001 *The Wanderer* is named a Newbery Honor Book.

2001 *A Fine, Fine School* is published.

2001 *Love That Dog* is published.

2002 *Ruby Holler* is published.

2003 *Granny Torrelli Makes Soup* is published.

2004 *Heartbeat* is published.

2004 *A Baby in a Basket: New Baby Songs* is published.

Selected Reviews from *School Library Journal*

Absolutely Normal Chaos
(1995)

Gr 6–9—Creech's newest story is told as a summer journal begrudgingly started as an English assignment. Mary Lou, 13, wonders if kisses with boys taste like chicken; if her best friend will ever shut up about her new boyfriend; and how visiting cousin, Carl Ray, can be such a silent clod, especially when someone has anonymously given him $5,000. Later, when he is in a coma following a car accident, she rereads her journal and wonders how she could have been so unseeing. Mary Lou is a typical teen whose acquaintance with the sadder parts of life is cushioned by a warm energetic family. Her entertaining musings on Homer, Shakespeare, and Robert Frost are drawn in nifty parallels to what is happening in her own life. When forbidden by her mother to say "God," "stupid," and "stuff," she makes a trek to the thesaurus to create some innovative interjections. Creech's dialogue is right on target. Her characterization is nicely done also. By comparison, this book is differently voiced than *Walk Two Moons* (HarperCollins, 1994), lacks that book's masterful imagery, and is more superficial in theme; but appropriately so. Creech has remained true to Mary Lou, who is a different narrator, and one who will win many fans of her own. Those in search of a light, humorous read will find it; those in search of something a little deeper will also be rewarded.

Bloomability (1998)

Gr 5–8—This honest, hopeful slice of adolescent life successfully explores how Domenica Santolina Doone, known as Dinnie, comes to terms with her past and establishes a secure identity for the future. Creech's skill at character development and subtle, effective use of metaphor shine in this first-person narrative with crisp, appropriately titled chapters. Deliberately, Creech introduces Dinnie as somewhat of a nonentity. Readers don't learn much about the specifics of her family life, only that her older sister and brother tend to get into various kinds of trouble, and that her parents are always looking for a new "opportunity" in some other town. By the second chapter, Dinnie explains that she's been "kidnapped" by her Aunt Sandy and Uncle Max, who take her with them to Switzerland to attend the school where Max is headmaster. In Dinnie's "second life" in Europe, her family continues to neglect her, forgetting even to let her know where they've relocated. Dinnie gradually adjusts to her new environment as she makes friends with other students from around the world: exuberant Guthrie; bitter Lila; and language-mangling Keisuke, who says "bloomable" when he means "possible." Together, these middle schoolers share classes and adventures, and explore ideas and emotions. As she reflects on her friends, her kind uncle and aunt, and her own vivid dreams, the youngster no longer sees herself as "Dinnie the dot in my bubble." Everyone can relate to the hard struggles of life, but, as the heroine comes to realize, the world is still full of "bloomability."

Chasing Redbird
(1997)

Gr 5–8—Creech returns to Appalachia in this story of 13-year-old Zinny, a middle school child struggling to find and accept herself plus look for a way to come to terms with the death of her beloved Aunt Jessie and her feelings of responsibility for that death. The novel revolves around an old overgrown trail that Zinny discovers and proceeds to resurrect. Meanwhile, her admirer, Jake Boone, is persistent about bringing her presents yet fails to convince her he is not really losing touch with reality after his wife's death, and guilt rooted in the past resurfaces to confuse Zinny, who comes to feel that the trail she is uncovering will somehow bring sanity, safety, and a sense of identity to her life. It does, but in ways she could have never have predicted. The journey for Zinny and readers is intriguing, delightful, and touching. Reminiscent of many novels about the rural South with wonderfully quirky characters and a focus on the setting of the natural world, this story seems much fresher and tangibly more in the present than most. Not as complex as Creech's *Walk Two Moons* (Harper-Collins, 1994), there is still plenty to discuss such as the symbolism of the redbird in the title and the ethical issues surrounding Jake's gifts and Zinny's mistrust of his affection for her.

Granny Torrelli Makes Soup
(2003)

Gr 4–7—Tastes and smells emerge along with wisdom and insight as a grandmother and grandchild reveal experiences past and present in the warmth of the kitchen. Rosie and Bailey are neighbors, born only a week apart. They are like sister and brother, only better "because I chose him and he chose me." She has always been his helper as he was born visually impaired. But now they have had a falling out. As Rosie tells Granny, Bailey is acting spiteful, all because she tried to be just like him. To be just like Bailey—her buddy, her pal—Rosie secretly learned to read Braille and unknowingly took away the special thing only he could do. When the two of them come together with Granny Torrelli in the kitchen and make cavatelli, the rift between them heals. Stories and wisdom continue as sauce and meatballs are made, helping to clarify feelings. As family and friends raise a glass of water to toast the cooks, Rosie realizes that her world is indeed bigger as is Bailey's; that *tutto va bene*—all is well! Twelve-year-old Rosie's narration seamlessly integrates Granny Torrelli's stories and fleeting conversations in short chapters. Her authentic voice gradually reveals what has happened and the accompanying emotions ranging from anger and angst to happiness and contentment. The integration of the Italian kitchen and Granny's family stories from the old country add flavor just like the ingredients in her recipes. This is a meal that should not be missed.

Heartbeat
(2004)

Gr 4–7—A tenderhearted story told in spare, free-verse poems. Annie, 12, takes great pleasure in running, but has no interest in racing or becoming a member of a team. For her, the pure joy comes from feeling the earth between her bare feet and the wind in her face. The experience is totally different for her moody friend and running partner, Max. For him, running is a way to escape his personal problems. Annie's comfortable, tightly knit world begins to unravel when she learns that her mother is pregnant and she becomes increasingly aware that her beloved Grandpa, a former champion racer, is slipping into dementia. She is a resourceful, self-possessed kid who takes comfort in the familiar but is able to face change and take it in stride. She marvels at the new life taking shape in her midst (her father provides month-by-month summations of the baby's development) and mourns the loss of her grandfather's strong and nurturing wisdom. School, art class, and chores appear throughout the verses, creating an everyday rhythm that matches the footfalls of this engaging heroine who loves to move, but who is willing to stop and smell the roses. Readers will enjoy meeting Annie, her family, and friends and will appreciate her resilience and spirit. This is vintage Creech, and its richness lies in its sheer simplicity.

Love That Dog
(2001)

Gr 4–8—Jack keeps a journal for his teacher, a charming, spare free-verse monologue that begins: "I don't want to/because boys/don't write poetry./Girls do." But his curiosity grows quickly as Miss Stretchberry feeds the class a varied menu of intriguing poems starting with William Carlos Williams's "The Red Wheelbarrow," which con-fuses Jack at first. Gradually, he begins to see connections between his personal experiences and the poetry of William Blake, Robert Frost, and others, and Creech's compellingly simple plot about love and loss begins to emerge. Jack is timid about the first poems he writes, but with the obvious encouragement and prodding of his masterful teacher, he gains the courage to claim them as his own in the classroom displays. When he is introduced to "Love That Boy" by Walter

Dean Myers, he makes an exuberant leap of understanding. "MARCH 14/That was the best best best BEST/poem/you read yesterday/by Mr. Walter Dean Myers/the best best BEST poem/ever./I am sorry/I took the book home/without asking./I only got/one spot/on it./That's why/the page is torn./I tried to get the spot/out." All the threads of the story are pulled together in Jack's final poem, "Love That Dog (Inspired by Walter Dean Myers)." Creech has created a poignant, funny picture of a child's encounter with the power of poetry. Readers may have a similar experience because all of the selections mentioned in the story are included at the end. The book is a tiny treasure.

Ruby Holler
(2002)

Gr 4–6—Orphaned twins from Dallas and Florida have resigned to living within the confines of the Boxton Creek Home for Children. It's a loveless existence. The Trepids, owners and "rule enforcers" of the home, target the brother and sister at every opportunity and all of the prospective adoptive parents have returned them to the orphanage. Eventually the children are sent to act as temporary companions to an eccentric older couple who live in Ruby Holler, and there they find love and acceptance. While the plot is predictable, the story weaves in an interesting mix of mystery, adventure, and humor, along with age-old and modern problems. Creech does a fine job of developing the unique personalities and the sibling relationship, and the children's defense mechanisms (Dallas's dreamy escapism and Florida's aggression) figure prominently in the interplay among the characters. The text is lively and descriptive with an authentic, if somewhat mystical, rural ambience. This entertaining read from a first-rate author will not disappoint Creech's many fans.

Walk Two Moons (1994)

Gr 6–9—An engaging story of love and loss, told with humor and suspense. Thirteen-year-old Salamanca Tree Hiddle's mother leaves home suddenly on a spiritual quest, vowing to return, but can't keep her promise. The girl and her father leave their farm in Kentucky and move to Ohio, where Sal meets Phoebe Winterbottom, also 13. While Sal accompanies her eccentric grandparents on a six-day drive to Idaho to retrace her mother's route, she entertains them with the tale of Phoebe, whose mother has also left home. While this story-within-a-story is a potentially difficult device, in the hands of this capable author it works well to create suspense, keep readers' interest, and draw parallels between the situations and reactions of the two girls. Sal's emotional journey through the grieving process—from denial to anger and finally to acceptance—is depicted realistically and with feeling. Indeed, her initial confusion and repression of the truth are mirrored in the book; even readers are unaware until near the end, that Sal's mother has died. Phoebe's mother does return home, bringing with her a son previously unknown to her family, who is accepted with alacrity. Overall, a richly layered novel about real and metaphorical journeys.

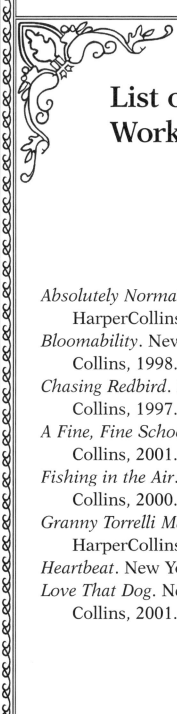

List of Selected Works

Absolutely Normal Chaos. New York, NY: HarperCollins, 1995.

Bloomability. New York, NY: Harper-Collins, 1998.

Chasing Redbird. New York, NY: Harper-Collins, 1997.

A Fine, Fine School. New York, NY: Harper-Collins, 2001.

Fishing in the Air. New York, NY: Harper-Collins, 2000.

Granny Torrelli Makes Soup. New York, NY: HarperCollins, 2003.

Heartbeat. New York, NY: HarperCollins, 2004.

Love That Dog. New York, NY: Harper-Collins, 2001.

Pleasing the Ghost. New York, NY: Harper-Collins, 1996.

Ruby Holler. New York, NY: HarperCollins, 2002.

Walk Two Moons. New York, NY: Harper-Collins, 1994.

The Wanderer. New York, NY: Harper-Collins, 2000.

List of Selected Awards

Chasing Redbird (1997)
American Library's Association's (ALA) Best
    Books for Young Adults (1998)
Parents' Choice Gold Award (1997)

Granny Torrelli Makes Soup (2003)
Parents' Choice Award Winner (2003)

Love That Dog (2001)
American Library Association (ALA) Notable
    Children's Books (2002)
Christopher Award (2002)
School Library Journal (SLJ) Best Books (2001)

Ruby Holler (2002)
American Library Association (ALA) Notable
    Children's Books (2003)

CILIP Carnegie Medal (2003)
School Library Journal (SLJ) Best Books (2002)

Walk Two Moons (1994)
American Library Association (ALA) Notable
    Children's Books (1995)
Newbery Medal, American Library Association
    (ALA) (1995)

The Wanderer (2000)
American Library Association (ALA) Notable
    Children's Books (2001)
Christopher Award (2001)
Newbery Honor Book, American Library
    Association (ALA) (2001)
School Library Journal (SLJ) Best Books (2001)

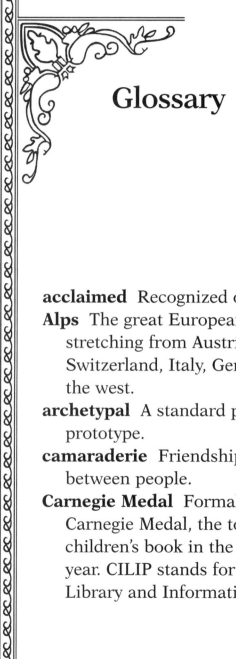

Glossary

acclaimed Recognized or applauded.

Alps The great European mountain range stretching from Austria in the east through Switzerland, Italy, Germany, and France in the west.

archetypal A standard pattern or model; a prototype.

camaraderie Friendship and support between people.

Carnegie Medal Formally called the CILIP Carnegie Medal, the top prize awarded to a children's book in the United Kingdom each year. CILIP stands for Chartered Institute of Library and Information Professionals.

chapter book A book with short chapters written for beginning to intermediate readers.

Chaucer, Geoffrey Considered one of the most important English authors, Chaucer lived from approximately 1340 to 1400. His most important work was *The Canterbury Tales*.

Christopher Award An annual award given to films, TV shows, adult books, and children's books that affirm the highest values of the human spirit.

contemplative Referring to a state of mind in which a person ponders thoughtfully.

Congressional Quarterly A Washington, D.C., news magazine that reports the up-to-date activities of the U.S. Congress.

deteriorate To become worse in function or appearance.

dysfunctional Functioning incorrectly; not working properly.

embellish To make a story more interesting by adding fictional, or made-up, details.

epiphanies Sudden realizations of meaning or reality.

Federal Theater Project Archives A collection of plays and materials related to the Federal Theater Project, begun during the Great Depression by President Franklin Roosevelt to organize and produce theater events.

free verse A type of poem composed of a variety of rhymed lines without a fixed rhythmical pattern.

Gardner, John A well-known American novelist and teacher who lived from 1933 to 1982, whose works include *Nickel Mountain* and *The Art of Fiction*.

heritage A cultural tradition and body of knowledge that is handed down from past generations.

literal Restricted to the exact stated meaning of a word or phrase.

Lowry, Lois The two-time Newbery Medal–winning American author of more than twenty novels for children and young adults, including *The Giver* (1994) and *Number the Stars* (1989). Born in 1937.

lyrical Relating to prose written in poetic, rhythmic language.

manuscript The handwritten or typewritten copy of a story before it is published.

Myers, Walter Dean A poet and author of many award-winning books for children and young adults. Born in 1937.

Newbery Medal An award given every year to the most distinguished contribution to American children's literature. A number of Newbery Honor awards (usually between two and four) are also given each year to books that the Newbery Committee considers to be of special merit.

poignant Profoundly moving, touching, often bringing sadness.

protagonist The leading character in a book or play.

proverb A short saying, or adage, which conveys wisdom and experience.

revelations Answers; exposed truth.

reverential Relating to being honored or looked up to in a godlike way.

Shakespeare, William Considered by many to be the world's greatest writer, this famous playwright was born in England in 1564, died in 1616, and produced works such as *Hamlet* and *Romeo and Juliet*.

Stratford-upon-Avon The city in England where Shakespeare lived.

Thames River A river flowing through southern England from the town of Kemble through London to the Atlantic Ocean.

For More Information

Web Sites

Due to the changing nature of Internet links, the Rosen Publishing Group, Inc., has developed an online list of Web sites related to the subject of this book. This site is updated regularly. Please use this link to access the list:

http://www.rosenlinks.com/lab/shcr

For Further Reading

Authors and Artists for Young Adults, Vol. 21. Detroit, MI: Gale Research, 1997.

Bostrom, Kathleen Long. *Winning Authors: Profiles of the Newbery Medalists.* Westport, CT: Libraries Unlimited, 2003.

Contemporary Authors, New Revision Series, Vol. 113. Detroit, MI: Gale Research, 2003.

Drew, Bernard. *100 More Popular Young Adult Authors.* Westport, CT: Libraries Unlimited, 2002.

Lowery-Moore, Hollis. "Creating People Who Are Quirky and Kind: An Interview with Sharon Creech." *Teacher Librarian*, Vol. 28, No. 4, April, 2001, pp. 54–56.

Pendergast, Tom, and Sara Pendergast, ed. *St. James Guide to Young Adult Writers*, 2nd Ed. Detroit, MI: St. James Press, 1999.

Rigg, Lyle D. "Sharon Creech." *The Horn Book Magazine*, Vol. 71. July/August 1995, pp. 426–429.

Seventh Book of Junior Authors and Illustrators, New York, NY: H. W. Wilson Company, 1996, pp. 67–69.

Bibliography

ACHUKA: Children's Books, UK. "Sharon Creech" Web site. Retrieved, July 14, 2004 (http://www.achuka.co.uk/interviews/creech.php).

American Girl. "Who's That Girl? She's Sharon Creech." Vol. 9, Issue 2, March/April 2001, pp. 43–44.

Aronson, Marc. "When Coming of Age Meets the Age That's Coming." *Voice of Youth Advocates*, Vol. 21, No. 4, October 1998, pp. 261–263.

Authors and Artists for Young Adults, Vol. 21. Detroit, MI: Gale Research, 1997.

Bostrom, Kathleen Long. *Winning Authors: Profiles of the Newbery Medalists.* Westport, CT: Libraries Unlimited, 2003.

Britton, Jason. "Sharon Creech: Everyday
Journeys." *Publishers Weekly*, Vol. 248, No. 29,
July 16, 2001, pp. 153–154.

The Carnegie Medal Web site. Retrieved June 14,
2004 (http://www.carnegiegreenaway.org.uk).

Children's Literature Review, Vol. 42. Detroit, MI:
Gale Research, 1997.

Contemporary Authors, New Revision Series,
Vol. 113. Detroit, MI: Gale Research, 2003.

Contemporary Authors, Vol. 159. Detroit, MI: Gale
Research, 1998.

Creech, Sharon. Interviews with Alice McGinty,
August 23, 2004 and September 4, 2004.

Creech, Sharon. "Leaping off the Porch," *Origins
of Story: On Writing for Children*. Barbara
Harrison and Gregory Maguire. New York,
NY: McElderry Books, 1999, pp. 20–35.

Creech, Sharon. "Newbery Medal Acceptance."
The Horn Book Magazine, Vol. 71. July/August,
1995, pp. 418–425.

Creech, Sharon. Official Web site. Retrieved June
8, 2004 (http://www.sharoncreech.com).

Drew, Bernard. *100 More Popular Young Adult
Authors*. Westport, CT: Libraries
Unlimited, 2002.

Edwards, Eden K. Essay in *Children's Books and
Their Creators*, edited by Anita Silvey. Boston,
MA: Houghton Mifflin, 1995.

Gallo, Don. "What Should Teachers Know About YA Lit for 2004?" *English Journal*, November 1984.

Gallo, Donald R., ed. *Speaking for Ourselves: Autobiographical Sketches by Notable Authors of Books for Young Adults*. Urbana, IL: National Council of Teachers of English, 1990.

HarperCollins. *A Guide to Teaching*. Retrieved July 2004 (http://www.harperchildrens.com/ schoolhouse/TeachersGuides/ cushmanindex.htm).

HarperChildren's.com "Sharon Creech." Retrieved June 10, 2004 (http://www.harperchildrens.com/ catalog/author_xml.asp?authorID=11974).

Hedblad, Alan, ed. *Something About the Author*. Vol. 147. Detroit, MI: The Gale Group, 2000.

Hendershot, Judy, and Peck, Jackie. "An Interview with Sharon Creech, 1995 Newbery Medal Winner." *The Reading Teacher*, Vol. 49, February 1996, pp. 380–382.

Holmes Holtze, Sally, ed. *Sixth Book of Junior Authors and Illustrators*. New York, NY: H. W. Wilson Co., 1989.

Hopkinson, Deborah. "A Magical Place Inspires Sharon Creech's Latest Novel: Interview by Deborah Hopkinson." Retrieved July 12, 2004 (www.bookpage.com/0206bp/ sharon_creech.html).

Jones, Nicolette. "Children Need a Place Where They Can Spit." *London Times*, July 12, 2003.

Lowery-Moore, Hollis. "Creating People Who Are Quirky and Kind: An Interview with Sharon Creech." *Teacher Librarian*, Vol. 28, No. 4, April, 2001, pp. 54–56.

Pendergast, Tom, and Sara Pendergast, eds. *St. James Guide to Young Adult Writers*, 2nd Ed. Detroit, MI: St. James Press, 1999.

Raymond, Allen. "Sharon Creech: 1995 Newbery Medal Winner." *Teaching K–8*, May 1996, pp. 48–50.

RETN Media Center, *Vermont Department of Libraries*, "2003 Dorothy Canfield Fisher Children's Book Award Ceremony." (Video-cassette) South Burlington, VT, 2003.

Rigg, Lyle D. "Sharon Creech." *The Horn Book Magazine*, Vol. 71. July/August 1995, pp. 426–429.

Seventh Book of Junior Authors and Illustrators, New York, NY: H. W. Wilson Company, 1996, pp. 67–69.

Spencer, Pam. *What Do Young Adults Read Next? A Reader's Guide to Fiction for Young Adults*. Detroit, MI: Gale Research, 1994.

Twentieth Century Young Adult Writers. Farmington Hills, MI: St. James Press, 1994.

Stewart, Michelle Pagni. "Judging Authors by the Color of Their Skin? Quality Native American Children's Literature." *MELUS*, Vol. 27. No. 2, 2002, pp. 179–196.

Source Notes

Introduction

1. Tom Pendergast and Sara Pendergast, eds., *St. James Guide to Young Adult Writers*, 2nd Edition. (Detroit, MI: St. James Press, 1999), p. 195.
2. Deborah Stevenson. Review of *Chasing Redbird*, *Bulletin of the Center for Children's Books*, March 1997, p. 243.
3. Sharon Creech. "Newbery Medal Acceptance," *The Horn Book Magazine*, Vol. 71, July/August 1995, p. 421.
4. Ibid., p. 422.
5. Joanna Brod. "Storytelling Sorcery," *Metro Times*, Vol. XVI, No. 14, January 3, 1996, p. 44.
6. Hollis Lowery-Moore. "Creating People Who Are Quirky and Kind: An Interview with

Sharon Creech." *Teacher Librarian*, Vol. 28, No. 4 (April 2001), p. 56.

Chapter 1

1. *Seventh Book of Junior Authors and Illustrators* (New York, NY: H. W. Wilson Company, 1996), p. 67.
2. Ibid., p. 67.
3. "Who's That Girl? She's Sharon Creech," *American Girl*, Vol. 9, Issue 2, March/April 2001, p. 44.
4. Kirk H. Beetz and Suzanne Niemeyer. *Beacham's Guide to Literature for Young Adults*, Vol. 12 (Washington, D.C.: Beacham Publication Corporation, 2001), p. 110.
5. Sharon Creech. (Interview with Alice McGinty), August 23, 2004.

Chapter 2

1. Kathleen Long Bostrom. *Winning Authors: Profiles of the Newbery Medalists.* (Westport, CT: Libraries Unlimited, 2003), pp. 266–267.
2. Sharon Creech. "Leaping off the Porch," *Origins of Story: On Writing for Children*. Barbara Harrison and Gregory Maguire, eds. (New York, NY: McElderry Books, 1999), p. 22.
3. Nicolette Jones. "Children Need a Place Where They Can Spit," *London Times*, July 12, 2003, p. 6a.
4. *Seventh Book of Junior Authors and Illustrators* (New York, NY: H. W. Wilson Company, 1996), p. 68.
5. Sharon Creech. (Interview with Alice McGinty), August 23, 2004.

Chapter 3

1. Sharon Creech. "Newbery Medal Acceptance," *The Horn Book Magazine*, Vol. 71, July/August 1995, p. 420.
2. Sharon Creech. (Interview with Alice McGinty), August 23, 2004.
3. Judy Hendershot and Jackie Peck, "An Interview with Sharon Creech, 1995 Newbery Medal Winner." *The Reading Teacher*, Vol. 49, February 1996, p. 381.
4. Creech. "Newbery Medal Acceptance," p. 421.
5. Sharon Creech. *Walk Two Moons*. (New York, NY: HarperCollins, 1994), p. 1.
6. ACHUKA Special, Interview with Sharon Creech, January 1998. Retrieved July 14, 2004 (http://www.achuka.co.uk/interviews/creech.php).
7. Creech. *Walk Two Moons*, pp. 224–225.
8. *Kirkus Reviews*, June 15, 1994, Vol. LX11, No. 12, p. 842.
9. Hazel Rochman. "Salamanca's Journey," *New York Times Book Review*, May 21, 1995, p. 24.
10. Sharon Creech. Official Web Site. Retrieved June 8, 2004 (http://www.sharoncreech.com/novels/06/asp).
11. Ibid.
12. Lyle D. Rigg. "Sharon Creech," *The Horn Book Magazine*, Vol. 71, July/August 1995, p. 429.
13. Creech. "Newbery Medal Acceptance," p. 418.
14. Heins, Ethel. "Review of *Chasing Redbird*." *The Horn Book Magazine*, May/June 1997, p. 316.

Chapter 4

1. John Peters. Review of *Bloomability*, *Booklist*, September 15, 1998, p. 226.
2. Sharon Creech. *The Wanderer*. (New York, NY: HarperCollins, 2000), p. 277.
3. *Publishers Weekly*, Review of *The Wanderer*, Vol. 247, Issue 10, March 6, 2000, p. 111.
4. Meg Wolitzer. Review of *Love That Dog*, *New York Times Book Review*, October 21, 2001, p. 30.
5. Sharon Creech. Official Web Site. Retrieved June 8, 2004 (http://www.sharoncreech.com/novels/11asp).
6. Deborah Hopkinson. "A Magical Place Inspires Sharon Creech's Latest Novel: Interview by Deborah Hopkinson." Retrieved July 12, 2004 (http://www.bookpage.com/0206bp/ sharon_creech.html).
7. Carolyn Phelan. Review of *Ruby Holler*, *Booklist*, Vol. 98, No. 15, April 1, 2002, p. 1328.
8. Press Release: Sharon Creech Wins CILIP Carnegie Medal. The Carnegie Medal Web Site. Retrieved June 14, 2004 (http://www.carnegiegreenaway.org.uk/ press/pres_C_03.html).

Chapter 5

1. *Publishers Weekly*, Review of *Granny Torrelli Makes Soup*, June 16, 2003, pp. 70–71.
2. Sharon Creech. Official Web Site. Retrieved June 8, 2004 (http://www.sharoncreech.com/novels/13asp).

3. *Publishers Weekly*, Review of *Heartbeat*, January 19, 2004, p. 76.
4. "Who's That Girl? She's Sharon Creech," *American Girl*, Vol. 9, Issue 2, March/April 2001, p. 44.

Index

Rosie (character, *Granny Torrelli Makes Soup*), 62
Ruby Holler, 8, 11, 13, 57–60

S

Sairy (character, *Ruby Holler*), 11, 58, 59
Sandy (character, *Bloomability*), 50
Shore Elementary, 14
Sophie (character, *The Wanderer*), 52, 53
South Euclid, Ohio, 14, 15, 22
Spinelli, Jerry, 67
Stretchberry, Mrs. (character, *Love That Dog*), 55

T

Thorpe, England, 28, 53
Tiller (character, *Ruby Holler*), 11, 58, 59
Torrelli, Granny (character, *Granny Torrelli Makes Soup*), 62

V

Victoria Park Elementary, 15

W

Walk Two Moons, 8, 10, 11, 12, 13, 16, 19, 47, 48, 54, 59, 64
editing and publication of, 43
plot of, 41–43
reviews/criticism of, 43–44
and winning of Newbery Medal, 8, 45–47
writing of, 39–41
Walnut Tree Cottage, 28
Wanderer, The, 8, 9–10, 16, 51–54, 59
Watsons Go to Birmingham—1963, The, 67
Winterbottom, Phoebe (character, *Walk Two Moons*), 11, 37–38, 39, 41
Witness, 67
Wolitzer, Meg (reviewer), 57
Wreckage of Agathon, The, 25

Z

Zinny (character, *Chasing Redbird*), 47–48
Zolar, Ms., 18

Alice B. McGinty is the author of thirty-seven books for children. Her nonfiction books range in subject matter from exercise to tarantulas to biographies. Ms. McGinty, who had the pleasure of conducting an interview with Sharon Creech, lives with her husband and two teenaged sons in Urbana, Illinois.

Photo Credits

Cover, p. 2 by Lyle Rigg, Courtesy of Harper-Collins Publishing

Series Designer: Tahara Anderson
Editor: Annie Sommers
Photo Researcher: Hillary Arnold